The 3 Reasons Why Book of People

Inspire. Educate. Entertain.

By 3RW & Ryan Stabile

www.3reasonswhy.com

See more reasons for everything at:

www.3ReasonsWhy.com

The 3 Reasons Why Book of People

First Edition.

Dedication

For all of those who seek knowledge.

Table of Contents

Introduction

The human race and our insatiable pursuit of knowledge is a tale that begins at the dawn of time. For better or for worse, seeking knowledge is hardwired into the human brain.

In fact, our quest for knowledge has historically often gotten the human race into trouble from the very beginning. Whether it be partaking in the forbidden fruit or the inquisitive cavemen of the prehistoric period who had to *know* which dinosaurs were herbivores and which were carnivores through a fatal series of trial and errors, *knowing* and *not know* can sometimes mean the difference between life and death.

Yet, still, the human race persists in *knowing things.*

Once our ancestors had their food, shelter and basic survival necessities fulfilled, they had the luxury of kicking back to relax as they pondered the mysteries of the universe.

The human race's biggest nemesis on their quest for knowledge has always been that daunting three letter word: why?

Everywhere you look, there is a potential "why?". While it would be difficult to go through life and ponder "why?" at every turn, sometimes you need to just kick back, relax and ask yourself all of those little questions. Only by asking the questions will you find the reasons for "why?". Those reasons are the only way that the human race can grow, learn and evolve beyond a prehistoric caveman. Because the more you know, the more you grow.

At 3RW, we believe that there are no stupid questions, only superfluous answers. A thirst for knowledge should not be oversaturated, like the constant barrage of information on the internet, or teased with just a few droplets of wisdom that only serve to intensify your thirst. 3 reasons are all you need to answer any "why?" and *The 3 Reasons Why Book of People* is your secret weapon in the fight against "why?".

Find out more of the 3 reasons behind life's biggest and littlest mysteries at the world's largest source for knowledge, www.3ReasonsWhy.com.

3RW™
3REASONSWHY

PEOPLE

3 Reasons Why Donald Trump is one of the most important people in the world

Donald Trump is one person everybody in the business and entertainment industries is familiar with. He is a business tycoon, real estate mogul, TV host, and a very controversial person.

Here are three reasons why Donald Trump is one of the most important people in the world.

Reason 1: He is a business magnet

Trump's early beginnings in the field of business started when he worked with his dad in his office. He referred to his father as his mentor and learned a lot from him. He became a big hit in real estate, specifically in Manhattan and New York City. He is known for being the owner of the Fifth Avenue skyscraper, Trump tower, and several residential buildings including Trump Park and Trump Palace.

Reason 2: 2016 presidential race

Everybody was stunned when Trump decided to run for president of the United States of America. His candidacy sparked interest and lots of controversy. Trump has been very vocal with his stance on illegal immigration, going so far as to say that he would build a wall between Mexico and the U.S. He also insulted the military records of Sen. John McCain and had been in a constant debate with Forbes regarding his net worth. Today, his popularity continues to soar as the media showers him with attention.

Reason 3: The man behind The Apprentice

If being a real estate mogul isn't enough, Trump also invested in his very own television show, The Apprentice, which first aired in January 2004. The show earned rave reviews with its first season finale tallying over 41.5 million viewers. The show has three Emmy nominations and has 14 successful seasons. In 2008, Trump launched The Celebrity Apprentice, which received positive reviews from audiences.

Donald Trump is one of the most important people in the world because he is a business magnet known for his real estate ventures and TV show, The Apprentice.

3 Reasons Why Bill Clinton is one of the most important people in the world

Former president Bill Clinton is known for much more than someone who "did not have sexual relations with that woman". Even long after his presidency, Bill Clinton continues to have influence and power.

Here are three reasons why Bill Clinton is one of the most important people in the world.

Reason 1: He was former President of the United States

William Jefferson Clinton was the 42nd President of the United States, serving from 1993-2001. He was a politician from Arkansas and was the first President when the country belonged to the generation of baby-boomers. He was also the first Democratic President of the U.S. since former President Franklin D. Roosevelt to have won a second term. Some of his achievements include having the lowest unemployment rate, decreasing crime rates and contributing to the lowest inflation rate in the US for the past 30 years.

Reason 2: His post-presidency contributions

Clinton remained active in public after his term as President. He was the one who established the Bill, Hillary, and Chelsea Clinton Foundation, which helps improve global health and wellness, as well as creating opportunities for women and helping to prevent childhood obesity. The foundation also works with others to fight climate change. It has several initiatives, including the Clinton Health Access Initiative, Clinton Climate Initiative, Clinton Development Initiative, and the Clinton Giustra Enterprise Partnership, among others.

Reason 3: He overcame a scandal

Despite his great track record as a president, Bill Clinton proved that he wasn't safe from controversy during the Monica Lewinsky scandal. People will never forget the scandal that rocked White House during Clinton's term, but they sure have seemed to forgiven him. He was impeached by the House of Representative in 1998 after he had a sexual relationship with one of interns in the White House. However, the Senate acquitted him from the said charges. It's not easy for any politician to overcome any sort of scandal, but Bill Clinton went on to make some great contributions to the world in his post-presidency.

Despite the scandal, Bill Clinton is one of the most important people, not only in the United States where he served as President, but also around the world.

3 Reasons Why Justin Trudeau is one of the most important people in the world

Canada is fortunate enough to have a young, intelligent and overall good-looking Prime Minster by the name of Justin Trudeau. But Justin Trudeau didn't charm his way into Canada's Prime Minister's office.

Here are three reasons why Justin Trudeau is one of the most important people in the world.

Reason 1: He is the Prime Minister of Canada

Trudeau isn't the first in his family to hold a high position in politics because his father was once the Prime Minister of Canada. He followed the footsteps of his father, Pierre Trudeau, and became one of the youngest leaders ever to serve the country. He entered politics when he was elected in 2008 to the Canadian Parliament, representing the district of Montreal's Papineau. He then became the Liberal Party's leader in 2013 and in 2015 he was elected as Prime Minister.

Reason 2: He was a teacher

Long before he became Prime Minister, Trudeau was a teacher. He graduated from McGill in 1994 and finished an education program from the University of British Columbia and taught French and Math in Vancouver. He taught for several years in the West Coast until he decided to go back to his home in Quebec where he intended to settle down.

Reason 3: Not your ordinary Prime Minister

Trudeau had many stints when he was still a young man. He was once a snowboarding instructor and a nightclub bouncer. He served as a rafting guide and camp counselor too. His good looks and talent in acting landed him the role of Talbot Papineau in a TV movie entitled The Great War which was aired in 2007. He is married to Canadian TV host Sophie Gregoire. As we can see, Justin Trudeau is anything but your average Prime Minister.

3 Reasons Why Satya Nadella is one of the most important people in the world

Professionals in the world of technology are considered some of the most influential and important people in the world because of their contribution to making life easier for all of us. Satya Nadella is one of these individuals who will forever leave his mark on improving the lives of many.

Here are three reasons why Satya Nadella is one of the most important people in the world.

Reason 1: He is the CEO of Microsoft

Satya Nadella is known in the tech industry as the Chief Executive Officer of the highly acclaimed Microsoft Company. He succeeded Steve Ballmer after a five-month hunt for the next CEO. Many critics believed he was the perfect choice especially after some stiff competition with other companies like Samsung and Apple. He kept Microsoft's sales from plummeting by making some brave decisions and driving culture change within company.

Reason 2: He is an achiever

The moment Nadella stepped in as CEO, he showed everybody that he is capable of great things. He was awarded the prestigious Champion of Change in 2015 and in 2014 he was also awarded the CNN-IBN Indian of the Year Global Indian. It was under his leadership that Microsoft unveiled its Windows Phone 8.1 and launched the latest operating system, Windows 10.

Reason 3: He is a millionaire

As CEO of one of the top performing tech companies in the world, Nadella has a salary to match his job description. In fact, Business Insider revealed that he earns a base salary of $918,917. He also receives a cash bonus amounting to $3.6 million and stock worth $59.2 million as part of his promotion, which he can only cash out in 2019. Not only that, but Nadella was also given $3.5 million last August 2013 to stick around while the company was searching for a new CEO.

3 Reasons Why Ginni Rometty is one of the most important people in the world

Tech giant IBM has been through a lot during the past few years. Competition is stiff in the industry and while others continue to rise, the company is struggling in boosting its profit margins. In 2012, IBM named its first ever female CEO in the person of Ginni Rometty.

Here are the reasons why Ginni Rometty is one of the most important people in the world.

Reason 1: She is the CEO of IBM

Many were surprised when IBM chose a woman to take over the company as CEO but Rometty proved to everybody that she was the right person for the job. Under her leadership, the company spent more on programs like cloud computing, data analysis software, and Watson artificial intelligence. The company also sold businesses that earned it billions of dollars but in the end, IBM either lost or just broke even in its ventures.

Reason 2: Fortune's Most Powerful Woman

Ginni Rometty is not just an ordinary face in the tech industry. She is one of the most powerful women in Fortune's list. As the CEO of IBM, her net worth is approximately $45 million. Moreover, she was also included in Time Magazine's list of most influential people around the world in 2012. She also has restricted stock awards totaling to $11 million.

Reason 3: Started working with IBM at 24

Rometty isn't new in the IBM family because she started working for this tech giant in 1981 in Detroit, Michigan. Prior to her position as CEO, she already held several leadership positions in the company. She was once the Senior Vice President and Group Executive wherein she pioneered the expansion if IBM in various parts of the world. She was also the Senior Vice President for IBM Global Business Services and during her term, the PricewaterhouseCoopers Consulting was successfully integrated to IBM. Meanwhile, in 2006 she was awarded the Carl Sloane Award by the Association of Management Consulting Firms.

3 Reasons Why Elon Musk is One of the Most Important People In the World

With his figurative hands in several exciting and cutting-edge industries, Elon Musk has already, at 44, had a fascinating career. Here are the three reasons why Elon Musk is one of the most important people in the world.

Reason 1: Co-Founder of PayPal

Worth approximately US$12.3 billion and listed at #38 on Forbes' list of the World's Most Powerful People, Elon Musk is a South African born, US-based inventor, entrepreneur and engineer. The companies he has created, founded and co-founded include PayPal, one of the most popular global payment options. PayPal has become, since its founding in 1998, one of the most-used and trusted online payment options. The site offers secure transactions, with credit card numbers and bank account numbers hidden. Initially, PayPal was a subsidiary of Ebay, still one of its largest clients, and became an independent company in 2015.

Reason 2: Co-Founder of Tesla Motors

Tesla Motors, a cutting-edge automotive company dedicated to electric cars, was co-founded by Musk and others in 2003. The company is innovative and focused, currently creating charging corridors along some of the US's most popular highways and pushing for a more widespread use of electricity as a means of private transportation. The company is also attempting to change a long-standing tradition in the US of selling cars through dealerships; Tesla Motors wants to set up its own stores and sell directly to customers, which is currently illegal in the US. The ruling which affects this type of sale is being challenged.

Reason 3: Co-Founder of SpaceX and OpenAI

Space Exploration Technologies Corporation (usually called SpaceX) is a US-based aerospace company dedicated to reducing the cost of space exploration and, eventually, creating the technology, vehicles and other factors which will make it possible for humans to colonize the planet Mars. The company has, so far, created two launch vehicles, the Falcon 1 and Falcon 9, as well as the Dragon, designed to supply the International Space Station. Another Dragon vehicle is currently in development, this one being a manned version able to carry a crew. Musk has also founded OpenAI, a non-profit organization geared toward the development of new artificial intelligence technology. In addition to the creation of AI, Musk has stated that he feels strongly about the potential dangers of AI and, while aiding in its creation, also warns that it needs to be closely monitored to avert negative consequences.

3 Reasons Why Hillary Clinton is One of the Most Important People in the World

Popular as a First Lady and now in the running to become President of the United States, Hillary Clinton is a powerful political figure. Here are the three reasons why Hillary Clinton is one of the most important people in the world.

Reason 1: Potential First Female US President

Already ranked at #58 on Forbes' list of the World's Most Important People, Hillary Clinton was first known to the United States as First Lady, wife of Former President Bill Clinton. Since Clinton left office, Hillary has remained active in politics. Since announcing her candidacy for President again for the 2016 election, Clinton has been on an almost non-stop tour of the US, speaking out on many issues important to the people. If elected in 2016, Hillary Clinton would become the first female US President in history.

Reason 2: Long History of Life in Politics

While most current US Presidential candidates have some history in politics, Clinton's stretches back thirty years and includes both of her husband's terms in the White House. While some critics have said that one can't learn about politics through marriage, most US citizens appreciate that seeing how the country is run on a daily basis is an excellent "training ground" for the Presidency. Hillary has not been a private citizen (with a few very short exceptions) since the early 1980s when her husband was elected Governor of Arkansas. Although she always displayed an active interest in politics, Clinton obtained a Juris Doctor degree in law from Yale University in 1974.

Reason 3: Strong on Important Issues

Although she has voiced strong opinions on virtually every issue relevant to the 2016 campaign, Clinton is perhaps best well-known for a handful of platforms. For instance, She is strong on healthcare, pushing for options that would make it accessible to every family without penalty. She also wants to put an end to sexual assaults and rapes on college campuses, which has been called a silent epidemic.

Clinton is also extremely vocal about closing the ever-widening income gap in the United States. In recent years the US middle class all but disappeared, while the percentage of people living at or below the poverty level has risen sharply. Some have said that there is no middle class left in the US, just the poor and the super-rich. Clinton promises to close that gap and restore the middle class through a broad range of initiatives.

3 Reasons Why Stephen Schwarzman is one of the most important people in the world

If you have titles like "King of Capital" or "New King of Wall Street", you can count yourself among the most important people in the world. Stephen Schwarzman has all of the aforementioned titles, making him a powerful person in the world of investment.

Here are the reasons why Stephen Schwarzman is one of the most important people in the world.

Reason 1: He is the Chairman, CEO, and Co-Founder of Blackstone

The Blackstone Group was founded by Stephen Schwarzman and his partner Pete Peterson in 1985. They left Lehman Brothers to put up their own investment firm which during that time had only $400,000 on its balance sheet. After 33 years, Blackstone grew into a powerful firm with over $333 billion in assets and revenue of $7.6 billion. Schwarzman alone earned $570 million in dividends back in 2014.

Reason 2: He is called "The New King of Wall Street" and "King of Capital"

The Blackstone continues to rise through the leadership of Schwarzman. Today, it is bigger than and as reported by Fortune, its assets amounted to $157.7 billion as of September 30 which is higher compared to the $88.4 billion it had back in May 2007. With so much money to spend, it's no wonder that Schwarzman is also known for spending his earnings on lavish things. He has several properties including an apartment at Park Avenue, a villa in Jamaica, and estates located in key areas like the Hamptons and St. Tropez.

Reason 3: He is a philanthropist

Schwarzman is known for being an active philanthropist. He is a supporter of education and many schools. Last year he donated a whopping $150 million in the establishment of the Schwarzman Center at Yale University. He also founded the Schwarzman Scholars in Beijing's Tsinghua University in 2013. Further, he donated $100 million to the New York Public Library.

3 Reasons Why Mary Barra is one of the most important people in the world

If you think the automotive industry is only for men, then you're mistaken. General Motors has a powerful leader and she's none other than Mary Barra.

Here are the reasons why Mary Barra is one of the most important people in the world.

Reason 1: She is the CEO of General Motors

Mary Barra is the first ever woman to hold the position of CEO in one of the most popular automotive company. She made waves as CEO of General Motors after making some very bold decisions such as pulling GM out of countries where it's not profitable such as in Russia, Indonesia, and Australia. She faced many challenges on her first year as CEO including dealing with faulty ignition switches as well as handling issues regarding deaths and injuries in line with GM.

Reason 2: A brave leader

Barra first took office as CEO of General Motors on January 15, 2014 and she's also one of the company's Board of Directors. As CEO, she had proven her worth as the brave leader of GM. She helped GM become one of the global leaders in automotive technology as well as design. She's very strict with the quality and safety of every product by GM. Before she was CEO, she was the executive vice president for the Global Product Development, Purchasing, and Supply Chain starting August 2013. She also served as senior vice president for Global Product Development. vice president for Global Human Resources, and vice president for Global Manufacturing Engineering among others.

Reason 3: One of Fortune's Most Powerful Women

Fortune named Mary Barra as the topmost powerful woman in the world, thanks to hear role as CEO of General Motors. Even though her first year was quite a struggle after the company's profits decreased up to 26% in 2014. However, she was back in the game months later after sales on GM's expensive trucks as well as SUVs increased. She also participated in a viral Twitter campaign that promoted women in the world of technology.

3 Reasons Why Bernard Arnault is one of the most important people in the world

When it comes to luxury brands, LVMH is one of the first companies to come to mind. Thanks to the numerous luxury items this company is famous for, its CEO Bernard Arnault is now an influential and powerful person around the world.

Here are the reasons why Bernard Arnault is one of the most important people in the world.

Reason 1: He is the Chairman and CEO of LVMH Moet Hennessy Louis Vuitton

Bernard Arnault is the CEO of the world's leader in luxury goods, LVMH, since 1989. At present, he is overseeing 70 brands which include Louis Vuitton, which is the largest and most profitable brand of the company, Fendi, Bulgari, Sephora, and Dom Perignon among others. The company also has 3,700 retail stores. However, he got most of his fortune from his stocks with Christian Dior and LVMH. He has stocks in Carrefour as well as Hermes. However, it was in 1984 when he first started in the luxury industry when he bought a business including Christian Dior amounting to $15 million.

Reason 2: He founded Louis Vuitton

The Fondation Louis Vuitton by Arnault opened last October 27, 2014. This cloud-shaped space has an area of 125,000 square feet and is located at Bois de Boulogne, Paris. Frank Gehry designed it and it cost approximately €118 million. It will feature LVMH art collection and also the works of artists like Jean Dubuffet and Damien Hirst among others.

Reason 3: He is a billionaire

According to BORNRICH, Arnault has a net worth of $37.5 billion making him the richest in Europe and among those in the world. As owner and CEO of LVMH, he is a man of impeccable taste. He enjoys playing the piano and keeps himself healthy by playing tennis. He is also a big fan of vintage wines. Despite his very busy schedule, Arnault values his family more than anything else. He got married twice and based on his biography, he takes time to have breakfast with his two youngest kids.

3 Reasons Why Alisher Usmanov is one of the most important people in the world

Tycoon Alisher Burkhanovich Usmanov was born in Chust, Uzbekistan on September 9, 1953. At 57, he is one of the wealthiest businessmen in the world. Aside from his wealth, he is also known for his love for sports and investments in social media and e-commerce.

Here are the reasons why Alisher Usmanov is one of the most important people in the world.

Reason 1: One of the richest people in Russia

Forbes hailed Alisher Usmanov as one of the most powerful people in the world in 2015. The source of his wealth is attributed mostly to his shares in Metalloinvest, MegaFon, and Kommersant which are companies based in Russia. Moreover, he is also a member of the Russian Union of Industrialists and Entrepreneurs. He was also one of the earliest businessmen to invest on Facebook but he later sold his shares in 2013. He also has shares with Alibaba and reportedly invested $500 million in Xiaomi, leading mobile phone manufacturer in China.

Reason 2: He is a sportsman

Many aren't aware of the fact that Usmanov was once a professional athlete. He was an accomplished fencer who was part of the national team of Uzbekistan. Even now that he's a billionaire he still shows his interest in fencing by being the head of the International Fencing Federation. Moreover, he has shares in Arsenal Football Club. He said that his love for Arsenal can likened to how a man loves a woman.

Reason 3: Order for Services for the Fatherland Awardee

Usmanov is known for his bizarre philanthropic works. For instance, he purchased the Nobel gold medal of DNA researcher, James Watson, for $4.8 million only to return it to the owner. He also paid over $20 million worth of art collection of Mstislav Rostropovich and donated it to the Konstantinovsky Palace. He also bought a large collection of Soviet cartoons and later gave it to a children's TV channel in Russia. Because of his philanthropic works, he was awarded the Order for Services for the Fatherland.

Alisher Usmanov is one of the most important people in the world because of his wealth, influence, and power. He is a billionaire from Russia and a sports enthusiast. He is also known for his eccentric philanthropic acts.

3 Reasons Why Wang Jianlin is One of the Most Important People in the World

As one of the richest men in the entire world, Wang Jianlin is a powerful force in international commerce.

Here are the three reasons why Wang Jianlin is one of the most important people in the world.

Reason 1: Richest Man in Mainland China

Running one of the largest companies in China, Jianlin's business savvy has earned him spots on several Forbes lists. He is recognized as the richest man in mainland China (separate from Hong Kong), #68 on the list of the world's most powerful people and #29 on their list of the world's richest people. He is the first resident of mainland China to enter into Forbes' top 20 list of wealth.

The most current figures available list Jianlin's net worth at approximately US$28.3 billion, and his company – Wanda Group (Dalian Wanda) – is worth approximately US$86.15 billion in assets. The group controls several internationally known companies, including AMC theaters, one of the largest movie theater companies in the US. In addition, Wanda Group has branches in the real estate, retail and hospitality industries, operating 125 shopping centers and 68 hotels with all of the hotels having earned five-star ratings.

Reason 2: Diversified yet focused

While Jianlin has invested in things like soccer teams (Atletico Madrid) and general sports (Ironman Triathlons), his main focus appears to be hospitality and its many different branches. His biggest business branches are real estate, shopping, hotels and movies, the last of which he plans to dominate. His Chinese movie theater chain, Wanda Cinema Line, is already one of China's largest and enjoyed a very prosperous 2015 despite a shaky Chinese stock market.

Hollywood is the next big check-box on Jianlin's list. He has plans to acquire a Hollywood movie studio, with previous potential purchases including Lion's Gate and Legendary Entertainment. This acquisition would be a step toward Jianlin's ultimate goal, which is to create a brand which sticks close to its Chinese roots while, at the same time, becoming an internationally known brand on the same level of Walmart or Google.

Reason 3: Understanding of the Global Marketplace

Jianlin understands that today's world of commerce is truly global, and he plans to create a brand that is fully Chinese while at the same time fully global. This, he has stated, is why he is investing heavily in foreign companies – his own companies command a great deal of attention in China but are largely unknown to the rest of the world. AMC Theaters was a step toward globalization, and acquiring a Hollywood studio would certainly be another big step in that direction.

With his unique status as mainland China's richest man, a savvy understanding of all aspects of the hospitality and entertainment industries and an eye toward the future, Wang Jianlin is poised to do even greater things in years to come.

3 Reasons Why Carl Icahn is one of the most important people in the world

As one of the richest men in the US and an outspoken activist, Carl Icahn is a powerful voice in world commerce and politics. Here are the reasons why Carl Icahn is one of the most important people in the world.

Here are the three reasons why Carl Icahn is one of the most important people in the world.

Reason 1: An Activist Shareholder

While many people own stock in different companies, Icahn has made investments his career. He founded his company, Icahn Enterprises, in 1968, and has built it into one of the most important firms in the world of investment.

Icahn doesn't just use his financial power to make more money, however. He is widely known as an outspoken activist, using his stakes in various companies to push for a wide variety of causes. This type of activism is exceptionally savvy from a business standpoint since it allows a shareholder with a relatively low number of shares to create real, concrete change in a company they do not own. It's also an inexpensive way to do this, far cheaper than purchasing the company or a controlling number of stock shares.

Reason 2: A Recognized Investment Leader

Icahn is well known in the world of investing and has amassed a pool of wealth which earned him several spots on Forbes lists. Currently, he is #70 on their list of the world's most powerful, #22 on the Forbes 400, #31 on the global list of billionaires, #20 on the list of US billionaires and prestigious #5 on their list of hedge fund managers.

Icahn also recognizes the importance of diversification. If a hedge fund or any large group of investments is too focused on one sector, they can be in big trouble if that sector suddenly takes a plunge or the industry is damaged for any reason. Icahn has wisely spread his investments across a broad range of industries, with just a few being food packaging, real estate, casinos, auto parts, energy and railroad cars.

Reason 3: A Potential Future Presidential Appointee

Despite being highly controversial, some experts are already predicting a US Presidential win for candidate Donald Trump. Trump has hinted that, if elected, he would prefer Icahn as US Treasury Secretary. This is a huge vote of confidence in Icahn's financial savvy, whether Trump wins or not. Although he points out that he does not agree with Trump on all of his controversial opinions, Icahn has stated that he would take the position if the situation became reality.

As a savvy activist shareholder, a brilliant financial mind, and a potential future government figure, Icahn is a powerful figure in the worlds of both finance and politics.

3 Reasons Why Aliko Dangote is one of the most important people in the world

As one of the wealthiest men in the world and the very richest in all of Africa, Aliko Dangote is an inspirational figure in the world of commerce. Here are the reasons why Aliko Dangote is one of the most important people in the world.

Here are the three reasons why Aliko Dangote is one of the most important people in the world.

Reason 1: Savvy & Smart Business Choices

The African nation of Nigeria is classed as a lower middle income country by the World Bank. This is far from the third-world image many in other parts of the world have for Nigeria. The country has the second-largest stock exchange in all of Africa and well-developed sectors in communications, finance, transport and law.

Growing up in Nigeria, raised by his grandfather, Dangote came from a long line of smart business. Dangote followed in the family footsteps when he graduated from college, entering the commodities market. Securing a small loan from his grandfather, he proceeded to purchase commodities at wholesale prices and resell them at a markup. The company he founded, the Dangote Group, is now worth approximately US$18 billion.

Reason 2: Interest in Creating More Independence for Nigeria

One of Dangote's goals in his business choices has been to create a more robust economy for his home country and neighboring nations without depleting natural resources. One of his latest pursuits – an oil field that would help lift Nigerian dependence on foreign oil – does utilize natural resources, but is still in keeping with his "hometown" state of mind.

Reason 3: International Recognition

Due to the growth and power of his company, Dangote has found himself on several prestigious lists around the globe. Forbes alone has listed him several times, including #1 richest in Africa, #71 on its list of the world's most powerful people and #67 on its list of world billionaires.

Due to his smart strategy of sticking with a business in which he grew up, his international recognition as a powerful and intelligent businessman and his admirable dedication to his home country, Aliko Dangote is one of the most influential men in Africa and recognized for his talents worldwide.

3 Reasons Why Masayoshi Son is One of the Most Important People in the World

With a history that includes brilliant innovations and devastating losses, Masayoshi Son has a vibrant story.

Here are the three reasons why Masayoshi Son is one of the most important people in the world.

Reason 1: Early Recognition of the Future of Technology

Son, inspired by a Japanese McDonald's executive – went to high school and college in southern California, studying English and learning about the emerging field of computers.

It was during this period, while at the University of California Berkeley, that he first realized the future importance of technology. According to Son he realized, upon seeing a magazine article about a microchip, that technology would be a huge part of the future. From then on, he demonstrated an amazing talent for invention, coming up with a new idea each day. One of those ideas, a technological translation application, eventually earned the young entrepreneur one million dollars when he sold it to tech giant Sharp.

Son went on to found SoftBank, a Japanese company which consists of many different branches. Its primary foundations are in communications and the Internet, although it also features broadband, e-commerce, marketing, media, finance and tech services. Son himself is currently worth approximately US$12.1 billion, with SoftBank valued at approximately 2.8 trillion yen in equity.

Reason 2: Rebound After Significant Losses

Like many people who had a large amount of money tied up in the dot-com "bubble" of the late 1990s and early 2000s, Son lost big when the bubble burst. After losing a staggering US$70 billion – according to most estimates – he worked long and hard. It paid off, and he was able to build his empire large enough to buy back the company he had founded and, several years later, purchase Sprint, one of the largest mobile phone companies in the US. SoftBank is still going strong, with significant improvements and changes scheduled.

Reason 3: Philanthropy

Son is also known for his philanthropy and concern for others. One great example of this was his response to the 2011 Fukushima nuclear disaster. He set up a fund dedicated to creating a solar power grid for Japan, hoping to eliminate nuclear disaster as a future worry. Another example was his response to the devastating Tohoku tsunami and earthquake of that same year. In addition to donating US$120 million dollars to relief efforts, he pledged his entire salary until the day he retires.

While he may be an oddity, Masayoshi Son is an oddity of the best kind. His incredible insight into tech's early years, his dedication after a massive setback and his continued generosity are just a few reasons why he is and will continue to be an important figure in global business.

3 Reasons Why Enrique Pena Nieto is One of the Most Important People in the World

Serving as the current president of Mexico, Enrique Pena Nieto is a man of dedication. Like other leaders out there, he wants nothing but the best for his people and country.

Here are the three reasons why Enrique Pena Nieto is one of the most important people in the world.

Reason 1: Early Dedication to Politics

During a campaign for governor by a relative, Pena Nieto got his first taste of politics and realized that he wanted to become a politician. In the years that followed, he pursued that goal, serving as State Deputy from 2003 to 2005, as Governor of the State of Mexico from 2005 to 2011, and being elected President of Mexico in 2012.

Pena Pieto was just 46 when he took office. This made him young for the office by the political standards of virtually every country in the world. However, his successful stint as governor, which was positively viewed by most of the country, convinced voters that he was up to the task.

Pena Pieto's political party, the Institutional Revolutionary Party or PRI, had, in the past, been plagued by rumors of collusion and scandal. Pena Nieto's election helped do away with a great deal of these rumors, promising that he and his party were free of bribery, collusion with criminals and criminal activity of any kind.

Reason 2: Desire to Make Mexico a Safer Place

One of the greatest threats to Mexican quality of life is the presence of drug cartels, and the violence they have created. During his campaign, Pena Nieto pledged to decrease this threat as much as possible. He instituted brand new police squads dedicated to the search for missing persons and garnered a lot of public support when notorious cartel leader "El Chapo" was arrested and placed in prison.

Unfortunately, however, El Chapo escaped from prison and has yet to be found. This led to a drastic downturn in public support of Pena Nieto and his leadership. Despite the setbacks, Nieto is still behind efforts to curb cartel activity and create a better, safer quality of life in his country.

Reason 3: Plans to Improve Mexico's Economy

Another big issue for Nieto is the Mexican economy. Part of his plans for improvement included making Mexico an attractive place for large, foreign automakers to build factories, thus creating more jobs.

He also plans to open the country's state-owned oil company, Pemex, to the public. This would also create jobs, foster economic improvements and trade with other countries.

Though his presidency has been plagued by scandal and poor economic growth, Enrique Pena Nieto is still a vital force in the global political world. This is due to his dedication to politics, his desire for a safer country, his plans to revitalize the economy and much more.

3 Reasons Why Ali Al-Naimi is One of the Most Important People in the World

As a head oil minister in the world's most oil-rich region, Ali Al-Naimi controls and monitors one of the most valuable assets on the planet.

Here are the three reasons why Ali Al-Naimi is one of the most important people in the world.

Reason 1: Lifelong Knowledge of the Oil Business

Ali Al-Naimi was born in 1935. Just 12 years later, in 1947, he started working for Saudi Aramco (officially called the Saudi Arabian Oil Company). Already a huge company when Al-Naimi began working there as a child, Aramco is currently the world's most valuable business, with wildly varying value estimates between US$1.25 and US$7 trillion dollars. The company operates both the largest on-shore and off-shore oil fields at Ghawar and Safaniya, respectively.

Al-Naimi stayed with the business for virtually his entire career, working his way up the ladder and eventually ending up as CEO and president before being named as Minister of Petroleum and Mineral Resources.

Reason 2: His Influence is Virtually Unmatched

Due to a combination of his long oil career, his unwavering confidence in his decisions and his status as leader of the world's most valuable company, Al-Naimi has an influence over oil markets, policies and even stock prices. His influence is unlike anything most people have seen before. In one incident, he publicly expressed confidence in OPEC (Organization of the Petroleum Exporting Countries) strategies, oil prices rose the very next day.

Reason 3: He Recognizes the Importance of Renewable Energy

While it may sound odd for a life-long oilman, Al-Naimi realizes the huge influence of emerging renewable energy science. He has stated recently that fossil fuels (oil, natural gas and other non-renewable sources of energy) could become "unnecessary" before the middle of this century.

This could mean several things. He may worry about the availability of fossil fuels, which will eventually run out at some point. He may have been referencing the growing global demand for renewable energy.
The oilman was quick to add, however, that he fully expected oil to remain a dominant force in the energy industry.

Due to his leadership of the world's largest company, his current term as Oil Minister and his progressive views about renewable energy, Ali Al-Naimi is and will continue to be a strong force in the global economic world.

3 Reasons Why Alexey Miller is One of the Most Important People in the World

Running the huge natural gas company, Alexey Miller is an influential person in world economics.

Here are the three reasons why Alexey Miller is one of the most important people in the world.

Reason 1: CEO and Deputy Chairman of Gazprom

Since 2002, Alexey Miller has served as Chief Executive Officer and Chairman of the Board at Gazprom. Gazprom may not be a familiar name to many around the world, but their product – natural gas – certainly is. Gazprom is the largest company in all of Russia and the largest producer of natural gas in the entire world.

Founded in 1989 and headquartered in Moscow, Gazprom has a revenue of US$106.3 billion and a net income of US$1.3 billion as of the latest reports. It employs nearly 400,000 people and is owned by the Russian government. In addition to natural gas, it also has branches which produce petroleum and petrochemicals.

Reason 2: Plans for Expansion

Handling the company business with determination, even in the face of opposition, Miller is currently working on an expansion of gas pipelines into Germany. This move would be another step toward Gazprom becoming the European Union's (EU) primary natural gas supplier. The pipeline is not without controversy, however, as Gazprom is facing legal issues which revolve around anti-monopoly laws.

Anti-monopoly laws are designed to prevent any one company or person from holding all the options when it comes to a particular product or service. Imagine, for example, if Chevrolet was the only automaker in the world – anybody who wanted to drive a car would be forced to choose a Chevrolet. These monopolies are historically bad for consumers, as there are no balances in place to keep prices fair.

Reason 3: Legacy of High-Powered Allies

Alexey Miller's success at Gazprom should come as no surprise. His career is studded with high-profile names, both in Russia and around the world. During the 1990s, he worked in the office of the St. Petersburg mayor, which put him into contact with Russian president Vladimir Putin. He has also worked closely with Dmitry Medvedev, the Prime Minister of Russia. Such a legacy of working alongside some of the biggest names in Russia surely instilled in Miller a drive to succeed.

Thanks to his history working for and alongside some of Russia's most important figures, his plans for expansion and his capable leadership of the nation's largest business, Alexey Miller is a huge part of the global energy industry.

3 Reasons Why Lakshmi Mittal is One of the Most Important People in the World

One of India's richest people, London-based Lakshmi Mittal runs a highly lucrative steel company. Aside from being wealthy, he is also known for his philanthropic works.

Here are the three reasons why Lakshmi Mittal is one of the most important people in the world.

Reason 1: Leadership of ArcelorMittal

As Chairman and CEO of ArcelorMittal, Lakshmi Mittal is one of the most powerful people in the world when it comes to finance and construction. ArcelorMittal is the world's largest steel manufacturing company, with assets worth over US$99 billion. Mittal himself is valued at about US$9.1 billion, which makes him #8 on *Forbes*' list of the richest people in India. *Forbes* also listed Mittal at #55 on its list of the World's Most Powerful People. According to some sources, he is the wealthiest man in England, and the second-wealthiest in all of Europe. Other sources, however, dispute these rankings.

ArcelorMittal is a very new company, founded in 2006. The companies that make it up, however, are much older. The conglomerate was the result of Indian steel company Mittal Steel purchasing European steel company Arcelor. The company is a true multi-national, with its headquarters remaining in Luxembourg. ArcelorMittal ranked at #91 in Forbes' 2013 list of the world's largest companies, produces approximately 98 million tons of steel each year and employs about 222,000 people globally.

Reason 2: Influencing a Financial Superpower

In addition to running the largest steel company in the world, Mittal has a hand in the financial world as well. He is an independent director for Wall Street giant Goldman Sachs, a multinational financial company which handles investments, securities and banking. The company's market cap is US$85.6 billion, with a great deal more in assets under its control. It has been listed many times on Forbes' lists of the world's largest and most influential companies, currently ranking 88th most valuable and 32nd in assets.

Reason 3: Helping Indian Athletes Compete Globally

Lakshmi Mittal is famous for being wealthy and spending lavishly – he owns some of the highest-priced real estate in the UK. He also gives back, however. One of his most public philanthropic ventures was the Mittal Champions Trust, funded by Mittal in order to prepare Indian athletes for competition at the Olympic level. Reportedly, Mittal was disappointed with India's performance in previous Olympic games and wanted to fund a trust which would help promising Indian athletes get the training and other help they needed to succeed. The trust shut down in 2014.

Due to his leadership of the largest steel producing company in the world, his hand in one of the largest financial institutions in the world and his dedication to helping others, Lakshmi Mittal is and will continue to be a global economic force.

3 Reasons Why Robin Li is One of the Most Important People in the World

Chinese entrepreneur Robin Li co-founded the country's most popular search engine. He is also known for his very humble beginnings and despite the fact that Baidu is often compared to Google; he is determined to show the world that his brainchild is unique on its own.

Here are the three reasons why Robin Li is one of the most important people in the world.

Reason 1: Co-Founding of Baidu

Robin Li attended Peking University, studying information management, and later attended the University of New York at Buffalo, where he obtained a Master of Science degree in computer science. Just two years after obtaining his Masters' degree, Li created a search engine page ranking system called RankDex. He obtained a patent for RankDex, and later used the technology on his search engine, Baidu.

Baidu was founded in 2000. Five short years later, Baidu made its NASDAQ debut as a publicly-traded company. It had quickly become the most popular search engine in all of China, beating out stiff competition like Yahoo! and Google. Baidu also offers Baidu Baike, which is very similar to Wikipedia and complies with Chinese government censorship laws which prevent certain Wiki pages from being viewed. Currently Li is listed on Forbes' list of Most Powerful People in the World at #56, and is valued at US$14.4 billion. He is also listed as the 6th wealthiest person in China, and the 18th wealthiest person in the tech industry.

Reason 2: Determination and Humble Beginnings

While Li's family was not poor, Robin was definitely not born into wealth as many rich individuals have been. His parents were factory workers, and he was one of 5 children. Li's success can be attributed to a strong drive to succeed, which is actually quite common of people who grew up in less than ideal financial situations.

Reason 3: Not a Copycat

In an internet field virtually dominated by US-based Google, comparisons between the two search engines – and their connected sites and features – are virtually impossible to avoid. However, Li has always been very clear that while the sites offer similar services, they come at the issue from different viewpoints.

As one of the wealthiest individuals in China, Robin Li serves as an inspiration to those not born wealthy, through his examples of invention, entrepreneurship and a determination to create – not copy – his ideas.

3 Reasons Why Abu Bakr al-Baghdadi is One of the Most Important People in the World

As the head of one of the most prolific and violent terrorist organizations in history, Abu Bakr al-Baghdadi is a powerful – if negative – force in today's world.

Here are the three reasons why Abu Bakr al-Baghdadi is one of the most important people in the world.

Reason 1: Quick Seizure of Large Portions of Land

Abu Bakr al-Baghdadi is the self-proclaimed leader of ISIS. Far more quickly than could be accomplished through legal, non-violent methods, ISIS, the radical group which preaches a severe, twisted take on the Islamic religion, has seized a great deal of land in eastern Syria and western Iraq. There are other, smaller pockets of land in the area under ISIS control.

In the taking of this land, ISIS forces have driven out or killed those who are not already Muslim or who refuse to convert, in most cases killing those who refuse. They have also destroyed several historic sites, including several which have stood since ancient and medieval times. Churches, temples and mosques are common targets, with even traditional Islamic sites being destroyed. Approximately 20% of all the historic sites in Iraq are currently under ISIS control.

Reason 2: Stunning Acts of Violence

While the world has been described as "immune" to violence, thanks to video games and violent movies, nobody was prepared for the beheadings and other murderous acts which ISIS proudly displayed on video. ISIS has also bragged of the killing of children. Many believe that this level of animalistic violence is part of ISIS's power – they are unlike any other enemy the world has faced, which makes them more frightening.

Reason 3: Brainwashing Over the Internet

Another part of ISIS's – and therefore al-Baghdadi's – new brand of fear stems from their apparent ability to brainwash or radicalize previously peaceful, rational people – often using only the internet. While not all radicalizing is done online, a large portion is accomplished this way, with potential victims being contacted through Facebook, Twitter or other, less well-known sites.

Far from being admirable or inspiring, Abu Bakr al-Baghdadi is one of the most important people in the world today due to his leadership of what is, perhaps, the most frightening terrorist group in recorded history.

3 Reasons Why Michael Dell is One of the Most Important People in the World

With a long and remarkable career in the tech industry, Michael Dell is still going strong. This is especially true despite the emergence of many tech companies offering better and more affordable units.

Here are the three reasons why Michael Dell is one of the most important people in the world.

Reason 1: An Early Start in Technology

Dell was interested in computers from a very early age. By the time he was 15, in 1980, he purchased his very first – an Apple IIe – and promptly took it apart to see how it worked. Following his parents' wishes, he entered pre-med school at the University of Texas. It was during this time that he began putting together the real-world pieces of his literal billion-dollar idea – that personalized computers, sold directly to customers, would be popular.

By 1984, he was running his business, initially called PC's Limited, out of a condo. Just seven years later, he was named in *Fortune 500* magazine as CEO of one of the country's top companies – he was just 27 at the time, a record for the magazine. Now simply called Dell, the company specialized in customized computers which were sold directly to consumers without the middleman expense of a store.

Reason 2: Privatization for Freedom to Grow

Dell has been a publicly traded company since 1988. The company which Michael Dell began with just $1,000 was worth approximately US$25 billion when he bought out his shareholders in 2013.

While going back to a private company is not the most common move to make, Dell touts the virtues of privatization. This leaves Dell and his employees free to take the company wherever they desire. Given the company's growth since Dell bought it back, he had the right idea.

Reason 3: Philanthropy

Dell and his wife have a history of giving back generously. Their foundation, the Michael and Susan Dell Foundation, focuses on three primary needs. Childhood health initiatives seek to improve the overall health and well being of children, especially those in low-income households and urban areas where healthcare is less than ideal. Urban education initiatives seek to improve the educational opportunities of children in these same areas, where schools are often underfunded and curriculums lack the quality and depth of schools in more affluent areas. Lastly, their initiatives on family economic stability seek to improve the overall experience of poor, urban families, with the ultimate goal of improving quality of life through health, education and many other factors.

Due to his early interest and talent in recognizing the importance of technology, his confidence in following through with the idea to buy back his own company and the generous ways his charity helps to change lives, Michael Dell is an important world figure in tech and philanthropy.

3 Reasons Why John Roberts is One of the Most Important People in the World

Serving as the Chief Justice of the US Supreme Court, John Roberts wields a great deal of power.

Here are the three reasons why Roberts is one of the most important people in the world.

Reason 1: Chief Justice of the US Supreme Court

John Roberts' position is a very important one within the US system of government. The Chief Justice is the head of a total of nine Justices; the other 8 are referred to as Associate Justices. The entire Supreme Court is often referred to by "SCOTUS" informally in print, television and online news, with the acronym standing for "Supreme Court Of The United States."

Roberts has been referred to as one of the most conservative Chief Justices in the history of the Supreme Court. Conservative views are typically those which align more with Republican agendas, although the two have gone up against each other many times.

Reason 2: An Important Left-Wing Shift on ObamaCare

Although Roberts is generally identified as conservative, he did make a very influential swing into left-wing territory in 2012 when he upheld the Affordable Care Act, often referred to as ObamaCare. This gained him support from left-wing politicians, but anger from his usual conservative backers. The Affordable Care Act has run into many problems since being signed into law, which has made Roberts' decision a target for both criticism and support from different factions.

Reason 3: Right-Wing Position on Hobby Lobby

Another important Supreme Court ruling involving Roberts was Burwell v. Hobby Lobby. This case dealt with Hobby Lobby – a public company but one which is run by Christian owners – fighting for their right to deny contraceptive care to female workers on the basis of their religious views. In previous court cases, a public company has not been allowed to have religious views. This case represented the first time the Supreme Court sided with such a company, allowing Hobby Lobby to go against part of the Affordable Care Act. Like any controversial decision, the case itself and the Supreme Court drew both criticism and praise for all involved.

Due to the importance of the office he holds, his determination to stick to his sometimes-unpopular views and the importance of the cases of which he holds power, John Roberts is and will continue to be a very important figure in both US and world politics.

3 Reasons Why Sergey Brin is One of the Most Important People in the World

Born in Russia, Sergey Brin is the founder of one of the largest and most successful businesses in the entire world.

Here are the three reasons why Sergey Brin is one of the most important people in the world.

Reason 1: He Co-Founded Google

After immigrating to the US at the young age of 6, Brin went on to attend the University of Maryland, followed by Stanford University. It was at Stanford that Brin met Larry Page, with whom he founded Google. What began as first a dorm room and then a garage stuffed with computers and a homemade search engine is now one of the most valuable companies on the planet and the most popular search engine in the world.

Reason 2: He Started with Practically Nothing

Brin did not have the advantage of being born into a rich or powerful family, as many people perceive all wealthy people have had. Instead, he was an immigrant whose powerful desire to succeed brought him straight to the top.

When it became apparent that they had something truly special, Brin and Page began borrowing money. They borrowed from friends and family until they had put together one million dollars, which they used to launch Google in 1998. The search engine quickly caught on and began to surpass other popular engines of the time, including Yahoo! and AOL.

Reason 3: He Brings Technology to Regular People

One of Google's founding principles was to, according to their mission statement, "Organize the world's information and make it universally accessible and useful." An unofficial mission statement or motto, "Don't be evil," showcases the lighthearted approach the company take toward their empire.

Every feature of Google does what the mission statement advises. In addition to organizing the massively confusing amount of information available online, Google offers many free and useful functions that help make everyday life easier. These include their wildly popular browser, Chrome, as well as smaller functions like Google Maps and Google Translate.

Sergey Brin is an important world figure and inspiration, especially in today's increasingly blended culture, of a man who worked hard and thought outside of the box to create one of the biggest companies in the world. In addition, he helps ordinary people make use of the Web and did it all coming from humble beginnings.

3 Reasons Why Li Ka-shing is One of the Most Important People in the World

The Chinese are known for their extraordinary business skills and Li Ka-shing is no exception. As the Chairman of CK Hutchison Holdings, he is a very powerful businessman.

Here are the three reasons why he is one of the most important people in the world.

Reason 1: He Came From Humble Beginnings

As a child, Ka-shing's family fled china for the then British-controlled area of Hong Kong. After his father died when Li was 15, he took a job in a factory, making plastic flowers to support his family. In 1950, he started his own plastics manufacturing company, which he then grew into the largest manufacturer of plastic flowers in all of Asia.

Another potential setback led to Ka-shing's next important step. When he could not renew the lease on his plastics factory, he took advantage of low real estate prices (driven down by the 1967 Hong Kong riots) and developed his own new business site. This step took him into the world of real estate, where he again excelled. By 1972, Ka-shing's company was listed on the Hong Kong stock exchange.

Reason 2: He Realized the Importance of Diversification

From then, he has gone on to acquire a stunning array of different types of businesses. In some way, Ka-shing and his companies are part of everyday life for virtually everybody in Hong Kong and beyond. His companies – under the umbrella company of CK Hutchison Holdings – have branches in telecommunications, electricity, plastics, cement, construction, real estate, public transportation, hospitality, television, shipping, steel production, sea ports, banking and retail.

Reason 3: He Lives Simply and Gives Back

Li Ka-shing is far from what you may envision as powerful business magnate when it comes to his attitude, lifestyle and generosity. Instead of spending thousands of dollars on a single business suit – as many wealthy people do – he dresses simply. His watch is not made by Bulgari, Chopard or even Rolex, but by Seiko – a brand most working people can afford. In addition to his simple lifestyle, he has given back to the community at a level most of us can't even imagine – over US$2 billion at last count, mostly through his philanthropic organization, the Li Ka Shing Foundation.

Giving the entire world an excellent example of both business savvy and humble gratitude, Li Ka Shing is an important figure because of his business empire, the fact that he built that empire from virtually nothing, and the incredible amount he gives back through charity.

3 Reasons Why Doug McMillon is One of the Most Important People in the World

A very important figure in one of the largest and most controversial retailers in the US, Doug McMillon's actions have been highly scrutinized.

Here are the three reasons why Doug McMillon is one of the most important people in the world.

Reason 1: He Heads the Largest Company in the United States

Doug McMillon is the President and CEO of Walmart. Walmart, along with its bulk-buy company Sam's Club, comprise the largest company in the United States. Since becoming CEO, McMillon has ranked as #29 (2014) and #32 (2015) on Forbes' World's Most Powerful People list. Around the globe, Walmart employs 2.1 million people. 1.4 million of those people are in the United States, which means that Walmart employs a full 1% of the US working population. The company posted revenue of over US$485 billion in 2014, is currently worth a bit over US$230 billion, which makes it one of the most valuable companies in the world.

Reason 2: He Rose Through the Ranks

Doug McMillon was not born into the "royal" Walton family line, as have nearly all former Walmart Presidents and CEOs. Instead, he attended colleges in Arkansas and Oklahoma, graduated with an accounting degree and an MBA, and went to work loading trucks at a Walmart distribution center in the summer of 1984.

Over the years, McMillon demonstrated business savvy which set him apart. He began working for Walmart full time in 1990, was named President and CEO of Sam's Club in 2006, and spent three years running Walmart International and was named CEO of Walmart in 2013. While not quite an overnight success, this demonstrates an incredible determination to succeed, taking McMillon from stock-boy to CEO in approximately 30 years. His rise within the ranks of upper management – Sam's Club to CEO of the entire empire in less than ten years – is even more impressive.

Reason 3: His Leadership Represents Innovative Change

Even as it enjoyed huge profits, Walmart became a bit of a representation of profits-over-people retail for many years. The company was criticized heavily for using cheap, unethical overseas manufacturing, paying its employees low wages and crushing small businesses.

When he took over, Doug McMillon took on the difficult task of changing this negative image. He has instituted wage increases and plans to raise them even further in the near future, realizing that a company grows on the backs of even its lowest-level employees.

Doug McMillon is a powerful figure in both US and global business due to his rise through the ranks to become Walmart's CEO, his leadership of one of the world's biggest businesses and his next-generation thinking regarding fair employment and e-commerce.

3 Reasons Why Jay Y. Lee is One of the Most Important People in the World

South Korean business magnate Jay Y. Lee is called the "Crown Prince of Samsung" and is next in line to lead the company.

Here are the three reasons why Jay Y. Lee is one of the most important people in the world.

Reason 1: Poised to Lead the World's Biggest Cell Phone Company

Having recently surpassed Apple in regard to numbers of units sold, Samsung is currently once again the largest cell phone manufacturer in the world. The company is worth approximately US$2 billion and employs over 275,000 people across the globe. As the Vice Chairman of the Samsung Electronics, Jay Y. Lee is next in line to succeed his father, the current CEO, which means that a great deal of people and power are under his control now and will be in the future.

Already listed at #33 on Forbes' list of the World's Most Powerful People, Lee is viewed as the next great hope for the already-huge company.

Reason 2: Plans to Improve Samsung

Although it's a monumental task to take on, Lee is reportedly already planning several key changes to the electronics branch of Samsung. Included in these changes are reported to be simplifications to the complicated structure of its corporate branches, and urgings to think more creatively while still retaining the stubborn determination that has gotten them to the top.

Taking on even a small restructuring of a such a massive conglomerate is a big task, but insiders report that Lee is more than up to the challenge.

Reason 3: Innovative, Global Thinking

While Lee has been criticized in the past for not having the charisma of his father, he is becoming a very well-received public figure. His polite but quiet personality has served him well in negotiations, where he has been known to create deals that astonish even those in Samsung's inner circles. He is also thinking globally, which the company hasn't done much of since it became a household name. Thanks to his ability to speak both English and Japanese, he can create contacts in a different way than other executives at the company, and his thinking is definitely global rather than strictly Korean. This will most likely mean great things for the conglomerate, as recent history has shown that businesses which ignore the trend toward globalization usually falter.

Heading the largest cell phone manufacturer in the world, Lee is one of the most influential people in the global economy due to the size and reach of Samsung, his plans to improve both outer and inner workings and his forward-thinking attitude toward the future of commerce.

3 Reasons Why Larry Fink is One of the Most Important People in the World

Leading a financial group which he founded, Larry Fink is one of the least-known yet wealthiest men in the US.

Here are the three reasons why Larry Fink is one of the most important people in the world.

Reason 1: His Investment Management Corporation is the Largest in the World

BlackRock, the international investment management corporation which Fink co-founded in 1988, is the largest of its kind in the world in regard to the amount of assets under its management (US$4.3 trillion). When combining the money that it either controls or manages, that number jumps to over US$12 trillion.

Running a company of this size is a huge undertaking, and earned Fink a spot on Forbes' list of the World's Most Powerful People at #34.

Reason 2: Key Role in the Government Bailouts

A huge part of the Recession of 2009 was the failure and government bailout of several high-profile financial companies, including A.I.G. and Bear Stearns. BlackRock is now in the high-profile position of managing those "toxic" assets, purchased by the US government in an attempt to balance a failing economy.

These toxic assets total approximately US$130 billion. In addition to these, BlackRock monitors Fannie Mae and Freddie Mac (home loan and mortgage corporations), reporting on them to the New York Federal Reserve.

Reason 3: A Unique Wall Street Personality

While many people think of Wall Street tycoons as brash, loud and larger-than-life, Fink is anything but. In fact, outside certain circles, he's virtually unknown, wielding a great deal of power but doing his work largely behind the scenes.

In spite of this – or perhaps because of it – Fink has a unique reputation among Wall Street figures. Those who know him tend to trust him implicitly, which speaks to his long track record of honesty and smart money management. He is known for giving a straight answer when it may prove unpopular, another mark of his confidence and knowledge of his industry.

In a world of sometimes-shady dealings and bailouts, Larry Fink has stood out for years as a voice of reason. His management of a staggering amount of assets, his role in the government bailouts and his Wall Street reputation are just a few of the reasons for his unique status.

3 Reasons Why Rupert Murdoch is One of the Most Important People In the World

One of the world's most powerful publishing and journalism magnates, Rupert Murdoch's companies span the globe and bring us much of our daily information and entertainment.

Here are the three reasons why Rupert Murdoch is one of the most important people in the world.

Reason 1: Building a Global Information and Entertainment Empire

Beginning at an early age, Murdoch understood publishing. He watched his father, Sir Keith Murdoch, run newspapers and, after his father's death, took over the family business. He bought and turned several newspapers in his native Australia into large successes before branching out. His next stop was England, where he purchased several newspapers, followed by the US, where he eventually became a naturalized citizen in order to be able to purchase television stations. One of his most visible acquisitions was 20th Century Fox, now 21st Century Fox, an entertainment company.

The companies Murdoch owned were split, combined and split again several times. The current incarnation is News Corp, which is worth approximately US$15 billion and consists of, among many others, 21st Century Fox, the *New York Post* and HarperCollins Publishing.

Reason 2: Recognition of What Sells Newspapers

For better or worse, Murdoch demonstrated an early understanding of what sells newspapers. He took a very hands-on role at his newspapers, even getting involved in typesetting and page design. He also shifted the focus of those papers to a steady feed of sex, violent crime and scandals, understanding that these types of stories are more likely to sell papers than other, less "exciting" topics.

Reason 3: Surviving Scandal

Although it's been said that becoming news is the worst thing a news professional can do, Murdoch did just that and came through the other side relatively unscathed. A scandal erupted when it was alleged that some of Murdoch's companies had engaged in the tapping of celebrity phones in order to get exclusive information.

Despite the scandal, Murdoch remains today at the head of one of the largest information and entertainment empires in the entire world.

Regardless of what might be said about his practices, Rupert Murdoch had had an enormous influence over modern print, television and online news. His companies reflect his understanding of the importance of diversification, and his triumph over scandal demonstrates his determination to succeed.

3 Reasons Why Mukesh Ambani is One of the Most Important People in the World

Living in the most expensive home on earth as a larger-than-life personality in his native India, Mukesh Ambani built his fortune through several industries.

Here are the three reasons why Mukesh Ambani is one of the most important people in the world.

Reason 1: Quick Rise to Power

Ambani's "big break" came in a rather unorthodox way. He was studying for his MBA at Stanford University in 1981 when his father was granted a government permit to open a yarn factory. The company – Reliance – was very small, but growing very quickly, and so the elder Ambani asked his son to return home and help run the business.

Today, his company, Reliance Industries, lists oil and petrochemicals as its primary means of income. The company's approximate asset value is $US85.9 billion, with Ambani's personal net worth being valued at about $US20.7 billion. He is listed by Forbes as the richest man in India, India's #1 billionaire and #37 on their global list of billionaires.

Reason 2: Nine Years as India's Richest Man

When Mukesh Ambani was named Forbes' richest man in India, it was for the ninth consecutive year in a row. This is an impressive feat, especially when considered in the light of the country's economy. India is home to some of the worst slums in the world, and a large percentage of its children are underweight (a common marker of poverty).

Reason 3: Residence in the World's Most Expensive House

While it may be a cosmetic factor, Ambani's house is still a factor when it comes to his wealth and power. Rising high above the surrounding neighborhood, the house – named Antilia after a mythical island – is a masterpiece of modern architecture and design. Despite its lofty stature, the house is not without controversy.

While many admire the house, many also consider it a vulgar display, especially in a country as poor as India. Whether it is loved or hated, Antilia is a symbol of Ambani's wealth and power.

Thanks to his determination to grow his father's business, his long-standing reign as India's richest individual and his lavish residence, Mukesh Ambani is a powerful and recognizable world figure with assets in some of the world's most lucrative industries.

3 Reasons Why Dilma Rousseff is One of the Most Important People in the World

An important political figure in South America and the entire world, Dilma Rousseff is a controversial and fascinating leader.

Here are the three reasons why Dilma Rousseff is one of the most important people in the world.

Reason 1: First Female President of Brazil

October of 2010 witnessed a milestone in Brazil when Dilma Rousseff won the presidential election. She became the first woman to hold the office of President in the South American nation. Rousseff also won her second bid for office in 2014, and is currently serving her second term as President.

As might be expected for the first female leader of the world's 7th-largest economy, Rousseff has garnered herself a reputation for being tough. Some believe that she takes this too far, berating members of her cabinet in public, while others think that a certain degree of toughness is almost necessary for a woman taking on a traditionally male position. Her nickname of "Iron Lady" reflects this no-nonsense demeanor.

Reason 2: Taking on Difficult National Goals

One of Rousseff's main platforms while running for President was the elimination or significant reduction of poverty in Brazil. The country's issues with poverty are serious ones, even as the country itself enjoys the strongest economy in all of South America. Urban poverty is a big issue, but perhaps even bigger is the rural poverty of the North East section of the country. In the North East, many families are living well below the poverty line, with little to no access to everyday utilities like running water and electricity. In these households, up to 25% of children under the age of 5 are chronically malnourished, and many more children work to help support the family.

Reason 3: Call for Impeachment

Due to alleged involvement in a scandal involving bribery and the Brazilian oil company Petrobas, a call to impeach President Rousseff has been approved. The process is still ongoing, however, and there is a good chance that no actual impeachment will take place. Over the years, many presidents around the world have had impeachment proceedings and trials begun, only to remain in office.

Despite controversy, Dilma Rousseff remains an important and interesting figure in South American and world politics. This is due to her unique position as Brazil's first female President, her willingness to tackle widespread poverty and her unusual (albeit negative) impeachment scandal.

3 Reasons Why Khalifa bin Zayed Al-Nahyan is One of the Most Important People in the World

As ruler of one of the smallest – yet wealthiest and most powerful – nations on earth, Khalifa bin Zayed Al-Nahyan is one of the most important people in the world.

Here are the three reasons why Khalifa bin Zayed Al-Nahyan is One of the Most Important People in the World.

Reason 1: Importance of the United Arab Emirates

The United Arab Emirates is a very young country, being just 44 years old. However, it is one of the most powerful in the world. The nation has huge reserves of oil under its control – the most recent amount was 97.8 million barrels. Al-Nahyan is the ruler of this small empire, having risen to the position after the death of his father in 2004. His full title is His Highness Shiekh Khalifa bin Al-Nahyan.

The U.A.E. plays a key role in global business, due in large part to the high desirability of oil. A great deal of global commerce plays out in – or is directly affected by – this small nation. It is also a visually spectacular area, boasting incredible modern architecture. One example of this is the Burj Khalifa, named for Al-Nahyan and currently the tallest man-made structure in the world at 2,722 feet tall from tip to ground.

Reason 2: Chairman of Abu Dhabi Investment Authority

The Abu Dhabi Investment Authority is a sovereign wealth fund. Sovereign wealth funds are investment funds held by a state which invest on a global scale. As a comparison, the only sovereign wealth fund larger than Abu Dhabi's is Norway's Government Pension Fund. The ADIA is worth approximately US$773 billion. Its beginnings were in oil, and still rely heavily on the natural resource, although recent leadership has diversified holdings somewhat.

Reason 3: Philanthropy

With so much money at his disposal, it would be disappointing if the Sheikh did not donate regularly to charity. Thankfully, he does not disappoint, donating large sums of money to many different hospitals, charitable organizations and educational institutes. Some notable donations include the construction of a new critical care and cardiovascular wing of John's Hopkins Hospital in Maryland, with additional money being given for AIDS and heart disease research. Al-Nahyan has also created and donated extensively to the UAE Pakistan Assistance Program, cancer research, low-income housing options and more.

Al-Nahyan is and will continue to be a key world figure due to his leadership a wealthy, unique and powerful nation, his management of one of the world's largest sovereign wealth funds and his generous philanthropy.

3 Reasons Why Benjamin Netanyahu Is One of the Most Important People in the World

Politicians make up the majority of powerful and important people in the world. As Israel's Prime Minister, Benjamin Netanyahu proves to be a successful leader despite the economic and political problems the country faces.

Here are the three reasons why Benjamin Netanyahu is one of the most important people in the world.

Reason 1: He is the Prime Minister of Israel

Benjamin Netanyahu is the current Prime Minister of Israel. Although a geographically small country, Israel has been central to some of the biggest controversies of our time. The role of Prime Minister is, essentially, the leader of Israel. Although the country does elect a president (currently Reuven Rivlin), the position is seen as ceremonial. The Prime Minister makes most of the decisions and holds most of the power within the country.

As the leader of such an influential country, Netanyahu has had a very long run. He served first from 1996 to 1999, was elected again in 2009 and has held the office since, being re-elected three times back-to-back. Only one other leader, former PM David Ben-Gurion, the very first PM of Israel, has been elected this often.

Reason 2: He is Vocally Opposed to Iran Deal

The highly controversial Iran Deal, in the simplest terms, limits the amounts of bomb-making uranium the country may hold, brought leaders from around the world together to discuss the possible dangers and advantages of such a deal. Netanyahu vocally opposed the proposed deal, taking a rare side against US President Barack Obama and others. He maintained that allowing Iran to obtain more uranium would be a dangerous step. In July 2015, a deal was released to the public announcing the terms of the deal.

Reason 3: He is Dedicated to Improving Israel

Since his first election, Netanyahu has been dedicated to improving the lives of Israeli citizens, eliminating the near-constant fighting regarding Israeli-Palestinian borders, and other improvement-oriented tasks.

Due to Israel's position as the center of a great deal of political unrest, Netanyahu quickly became a name known around the world. Within his own country, he has instituted reforms and programs which were aimed at improving the quality of life in Israel, including (among many others) welfare programs, foreign investment legalization and the reform of banking systems.

Regardless of Israel's rocky past, Netanyahu is an important world figure because of his long leadership terms, his Iran Deal opposition and his dedication to Israel and its people.

3 Reasons Why Jack Ma is One of the Most Important People in the World

Chinese businessmen are among the most successful in the industry and Jack Ma reigns over all of them. He is one of Forbes' most powerful people because of his contribution to the business sector.

Here are the three reasons why Jack Ma is one of the most important people in the world.

Reason 1: He founded the Alibaba Group

While you may not immediately recognize Jack Ma's name (Ma Yun in Chinese), you're probably familiar with his company. Alibaba group has grown steadily since its conception in 1999, when it began as a business-to-business commerce site which connected foreign buyers to Chinese manufacturers. Today, the name encompasses several branches of business, including retail sales, B2B sales, wholesale, electronic payment services, cloud computing and a search engine geared toward shopping.

Reason 2: He has Side Ventures

While Alibaba Group is constantly growing and evolving, it has created some incredibly diverse and successful side ventures during its relatively very short existence. These include the Alibaba Pictures Group, an entertainment branch, AliExpress, a grouping of small business offering their goods to global consumers, eTao, which offers consumers an easy platform for comparison shopping, and Juhuasuan, which offers "flash" sales with low prices for short periods of time. Perhaps the most recognizable name in the Alibaba Group family is China Yahoo! - the email giant also offers news, shopping and search features. Although email was shut down and accounts switched to AliMail or another service, other Yahoo! services remain intact.

Reason 3: He Came from Humble Beginnings

Jack Ma is an important reminder that it does not take a high-profile name or family history in order to become a huge success. Ma was born to musician-storytellers and taught himself English by escorting tourists around his hometown, later earning several college degrees. He did not encounter a computer until he was 33 years old (he's currently 48) and does not write code. His empire was created through hard work and dedication.

Jack Ma is an important figure in today's global economy due to his Alibaba Group and its various branches, the side ventures owned by the group and the inspiring example he provides for all would-be entrepreneurs.

3 Reasons Why Christine LaGarde is One of the Most Important People in the World

In a world dominated by men, it's not often to find successful women holding high positions. However, Christine LaGarde proved them wrong after she landed "first female" positions in the world of law and finance.

Here are the three reasons why Christine LaGarde is one of the most important people in the world.

Reason 1: Head of the IMF

Since July of 2011, LaGarde has been the Managing Director of the International Monetary Fund. It was during this leadership, in 2014, that Lagarde was named the 5th Most Powerful Woman in the World by *Forbes* magazine.

The IMF, an organization of 188 countries headquartered in Washington, D.C., has several functions. It serves as a pool of money from which financially troubled countries can borrow if they need assistance. Each member country makes regular contributions to ensure that this option is always available. It strives to encourage financial cooperation between countries, create and sustain high employment rates and lower global poverty, among many other functions. The group was founded in 1944.

Reason 2: A "First Female" Law Position

Christine LaGarde is the first woman to ever head the IMF, but this is not her only "first female" position.

In 1981, she joined large international law firm Baker & McKenzie. In 1999, she was elected Chairman, marking the first time a woman had ever held the top spot in the firm's executive committee.

LaGarde's "first female" positions are even more significant because they came in the fields of international law and finance, two industries which have largely and historically been dominated by men.

Reason 3: A Previous "First Female" Finance Position

Another shining moment in LaGarde's career came in 2007 when she joined France's Ministry of Economic Affairs. This position made her first woman in history to lead France's economic policy.

She also took a stand against racism during this period in her career. Famed fragrance house Guerlain – one of the oldest in the world and headquartered in Paris, suffered a PR scandal when its former master perfumer Jean-Paul Guerlain, made racist remarks on French television. He was soon dismissed from his role as advisor. Christine LaGarde distinguished herself by being the only voice of condemnation for the remarks from the political class in France.

Christine LaGarde is an important figure in today's world because of her leadership of the IMF, her string of "first female" roles and her unique vocalization against racism in France.

3 Reasons Why Jeffrey Immelt is One of the Most Important People in the World

Jeffrey Immelt is a very popular CEO. He is the person behind the success of General Electric. It is through his leadership that the company was able to survive several crises, including the recession.

Here are the three reasons why Jeffrey Immelt is one of the most important people in the world.

Reason 1: He Heads a Multinational Empire

Since 2001, Jeffrey Immelt has served as CEO of General Electric, commonly known as GE. He also serves as Chairman of the Board. GE is one of the largest companies in the US, ranking 26th in revenue, 14th in profits. Overall, they are the fourth-largest in the world according to *Forbes*. GE was founded in 1892; world-famous inventor Thomas Edison was a co-founder.

Although most consumers are familiar with GE's line of home appliances, their reach is extremely broad, with divisions dedicated to oil, gas, energy, aviation, finances, medical services, pharmaceuticals, automotive components, software development, engineering, energy management and healthcare.

Currently, GE is valued at approximately $253.5 billion and employs approximately 305,000 people in the US and other countries.

Reason 2: He Helped GE in Surviving Crises

Immelt took over as CEO of GE in early September 2001, literally days before the terrorist attacks of 9/11. With GE's large aircraft engine branch taking a big hit, Immelt had his work cut out for him as CEO. Despite the unavoidable setbacks created by the attacks, he led GE through the crisis and the aircraft-engine branch is, today, a highly profitable one for the company.

Just a few months after the 9/11 attacks, the US economic market was rocked the Enron scandal. Virtually every sector of Enron was willfully corrupt, and the scandal prompted a very thorough investigation of nearly every major US corporation – GE was no exception. Immelt was able to show that GE's practices were above-board and legal, thereby carrying the company through another potentially devastating period.

Reason 3: He was behind GE's Survival during Recession

During 2008, the US plunged into the worst economic crisis since the Great Depression. Virtually all economic sectors were affected, including those in which GE had branches. They were part of the controversial "bailouts," receiving aid from the Federal Reserve, but managed to come through the Recession without the negative stigma which still haunts some affected companies and organizations.

Jeffrey Immelt is an important figure in commerce and finance because of his competent leadership of one of the world's largest companies, his confident guidance of that company through two back-to-back crises, and his survival of the 2008 Recession.

3 Reasons Why Rex Tillerson is One of the most Important People in the World

Exxon Mobil supplies the majority of the world's gas and oil products and it is run by Rex Tillerson. He is a native of Wichita Falls, Texas and holds a degree in civil engineering from the University of Texas.

Here are the three reasons why Rex Tillerson is one of the most important people in the world.

Reason 1: He Runs One of the Largest Global Companies

As of 2006, Tillerson has been the CEO and chairman of Exxon Mobil. Exxon is one of the largest gas-and-oil companies in the world. The company is ranked #7 on Forbes' Global 2000 list, #4 in sales and #3 in market value. The company is worth approximately $357.1 billion and employs about 84,000 people.

Exxon Mobil has a very long and historic past. It is the current incarnation of Standard Oil, the company started by famous US business magnate John D. Rockefeller. Rockefeller founded the company in 1870.

Exxon Mobil is currently the largest refiner (oil driller and producer) in the world. They operate 37 oil refineries in 21 countries around the world.

Reason 2: He Operates a Controversial Company

After the 1989 Exxon Valdez oil spill, one of the worst in history in terms of environmental impact, the company name has had a stigma. Other incidents, including a requested cleanup in Brooklyn, New York and a leak in Baton Rouge, Louisiana, have further added to Exxon's less-than-ideal perception among environmentalists. Taking on a company with this type of history has its own challenges.

Reason 3: He Successfully Rose Up Through the Company

Tillerson didn't become CEO until 2006, but he had already been at the company for thirty years. He began with Exxon right after graduating from the University of Texas at Austin with a Bachelors' degree in civil engineering. Over the years, he held several positions, including president of two foreign Exxon branches.

Rex Tillerson is an important figure in global commerce due to his leadership of one of the world's largest companies, his willingness to take on the leadership of a controversial company, and his inspirational rise from an entry-level employee to CEO.

3 Reasons Why Lloyd Blankfein is One of the Most Important People in the World

Lloyd Craig Blankfein is known for being the leader of Goldman Sachs. He holds the position since May 2006 after his predecessor, Henry Paulson, was nominated for Secretary of the Treasury. But what makes him so important?

Here are the three reasons why Lloyd Blankfein is one of the most important people in the world.

Reason 1: He Runs a Massive Financial Services Company

Since 2006, Lloyd Blankfein has served as CEO and chairman of Goldman Sachs. Goldman Sachs is one of the largest international investment banking firms in the world, with offices across the globe. In addition to investments, it also offers securities and investment management. The client list of Goldman Sachs is wide and varied, ranging from corporations, financial institutions and entire governments to private, high-income individuals. Its current value is approximately $86.5 billion.

Taking on any company of this size requires a special kind of individual. Throughout his entire life, Blankfein has demonstrated a rare skill set of determination, intelligence and outside-the-box thinking which made him perfect for the position.

Reason 2: He Survived the Recession

Goldman Sachs, along with many other financial services companies, was hit hard by the Recession of 2008. Companies were going bankrupt left and right, but Goldman Sachs did not. Instead, Blankfein sought out a way to turn the recession to his advantage. He utilized low competition and interest rates to Goldman Sachs' advantage and managed to survive the Recession intact. His bold moves earned him the unique *Forbes* distinction of "The Most Outrageous CEO of 2009."

Reason 3: He Is a Self-Made Man

When it comes to big business, we often hear of company positions being handed down from father to son. While this is technically called nepotism and is illegal, there are many sneaky ways to get around nepotism laws. Blankfein, however, has no high-finance background. He was raised in a New York City housing project and worked as a vendor at Yankee Stadium as a high school student. Despite his regular-guy beginnings – or perhaps because of those beginnings – he developed the skill set necessary to run a massive multinational like Goldman Sachs.

Lloyd Blankfein is one of the most important people in the world today because of his capable and intelligent management of one of the largest finance companies in the world, his strategic thinking during a very dark period for the US economy, and his inspiring rise from housing projects to Wall Street.

3 Reasons Why Tim Cook is One of the Most Important People in the World

Timothy Donald "Tim" Cook is best known for being the CEO of Apple. But aside from holding this position, he also serves as a member of the board of Duke University where he graduated in 1988, Nike Inc., and the National Football Association.

Here are the three reasons why Tim Cook is one of the most important people in the world.

Reason 1: He Leads One of the Largest IT Companies in the World

Late in 2011, when famed Apple founder Steve Jobs stepped down due to health reasons, he was succeeded by Tim Cook. Cook had been with the company since 1998 and had already held several high-level positions including COO – which he held until becoming CEO – and as executive vice president of worldwide sales and operations. A few years prior, he had served as acting CEO when Jobs was forced to take a leave of absence.

As CEO of Apple, Cook is at the forefront of technology in the US and around the globe. The company is worth approximately $741.8 billion and is #1 on Forbes list of most valuable brands in the world. They are also #1 in market value.

Reason 2: He Helped Reverse a Downward Profit Spiral

In 1995, Apple's revenue was approximately 11 billion. In 1998, when Cook signed on, that number was down to a discouraging 6 billion. Cook and Jobs reportedly made an excellent team, creating changes and taking risks which took the company from a struggling home computer brand to the tech giant which it is today.

Reason 3: He Took a Leap of Faith Which Paid Off

According to Cook, he was ready to sign on at Apple after his first meeting with Steve Jobs, despite the company's discouraging past and despite people close to him saying that the move would be a bad idea. He recognized, however, that Jobs was a visionary, and that to pass up the opportunity would be to pass up something extremely rare. Trusting his instincts paid off, as the company is now recognized as the most valuable brand in the world.

Tim Cook is one of the most important people in the world due to the size of the company he runs, the resurrection he and Jobs performed when Apple was struggling, and his amazing instincts which told him to take a risk.

3 Reasons Why Akio Toyoda is One of the Most Important People in the World

Toyota cars are some of the most popular in many countries, including the US and Canada. While they don't have as strong of a foothold in Europe, they are extremely strong in Japan and other parts of Asia. Today, Toyota is run by Akio Toyoda.

Here are the three reasons why Akio Toyoda is one of the most important people in the world.

Reason 1: Head of the Largest Automaker in the World

Toyoda, since 2009, has been CEO of Toyota Motor Corporation, the largest car manufacturer in the world. The company surpassed General Motors in recent years, as well as Volkswagen. They arrived at the milestone of producing more than 10 million cars in a single year during 2012, the same year they produced their 200-millionth vehicle.

Reason 2: He Shakes Things Up at Toyota

Although the Toyoda name is firmly entrenched in Toyota history, Akio Toyoda is not his predecessors. Instead, he seeks to create some major change within the company, all focused on improving their products. He is approaching this in several ways, including all-new production plants designed for productivity and efficiency. He is also focusing more heavily on the Prius, one of the first hybrid cars on the market and still a strong seller in the "green" car market.

Reason 3: He Reversed a Downward Slide

While Toyota has never been in danger of closing down, a few years ago their numbers weren't as great as they are today. Toyoda is credited with bringing the company back up into the #1 spot. A tsunami, recalls and a change in how consumers viewed Toyota cars all combined to damage the brand's reputation. Customers who viewed a Toyota as a "cheap" car were increasing, while quality was a word less – associated with the brand.

Toyoda sought to change all that, and by all accounts, he has and is succeeding. He has been, in the long line of Toyoda management, perhaps the closest to the actual work of building and designing cars since the company's founder.

Akio Toyoda is a strong force in the economic world today due to his leadership of the world's largest automaker, the fact that he shook up such a large company in positive ways, and because he rescued Toyota from what could have been a permanently damaging time period.

3 Reasons Why Charles Koch is One of the Most Important People in the World

Charles Koch's personal net worth of over $43 billion. This also makes him (along with his brother) the 6th wealthiest individual in the world – the brothers tied for the spot.

Here are the three reasons why Charles Koch is one of the most important people in the world.

Reason 1: He Runs One of the Largest Privately Held Companies in the World

Charles Koch holds three very important positions at Koch Industries – chairman of the board, co-owner (with his brother David) and CEO. The brothers inherited the business from their father, Fred Koch, who founded the company in 1940.

Koch Industries isn't as familiar to many consumers as some other companies of the same size and scope, but their products and services certainly are. They own well-known names like Georgia-Pacific, Molex and Invista, as well as many others. Koch Industries is a very diverse company, with branches in ranching, polymers, petroleum, energy, chemicals, fertilizers, minerals, paper, finance and more. Just a few Koch products which most people see or use every day include paper cups and indoor carpeting.

Reason 2: He is a Philanthropist

Through the Charles Koch Foundation, Koch gives back in many ways. The institute supports higher learning, giving grants to colleges and universities. Koch himself is passionate about free society, and a lot of his giving leans toward this goal. Due to these ideals, those receiving grants are free to use them as they see fit, without the "hovering" which is present with some types of grants. Academic freedom and independence are tenets which Koch holds dear, and he seeks to further these ideals through his philanthropy. Ultimately, the foundation seeks to help programs, universities and individuals who have a realistic chance of creating real change in their universities and communities.

Reason 3: He Seeks Transparency

In an era when billionaires are often demonized simply because they have a lot of money, Charles Koch tries to fight the "untouchable" image surrounding the very rich. His book Good Profit outlines the principles which have allowed the Koch brothers to grow their business to such huge proportions, but also includes funny glimpses of the man behind the billions.

Charles Koch is one of the most important men in the world because of his leadership at a multi-industry giant, his deep desire to give back and better the world, and his efforts to demystify himself as one of the richest men in the world.

3 Reasons Why David Koch is One of the Most Important People in the World

David Koch is tied with his brother for the 6th wealthiest individuals in the world, and 4th in the United States, with a net worth of approximately $43 billion. The brothers were also tied for the richest person (people) in their home state of New York, and are the 9th-richest people in the world.

Here are the three reasons why David Koch is one of the most important people in the world.

Reason 1: He Runs One of the Largest Privately Held Companies in the World

Koch Industries, which David Koch co-owns with his brother Charles, is the second-largest privately held company in the United States. This means that the company is not traded publicly. Stocks are privately traded, and the companies are typically run by a smaller group of leaders than publicly traded organizations. The Koch brothers inherited the business from their father Fred Koch, who founded it in 1940.

Reason 2: He Understands the Importance of Diversifying

Koch Industries is extremely diversified, and that diversity has long been one of the keys to their success. They have branches which manufacture items that many people use every day, including paper products, and products they use but are not usually aware of, such as the wood panels used to build most modern homes.

Koch Industries also has branches which deal with globally important commodities like oil, as well as products crucial to the infrastructure of the US such as cement and its components. Pharmaceuticals, minerals, commodities trading, finance, fibers, fertilizers and many other products also contribute to the diversity of Koch.

Reason 3: He Gives Back to the Community

David Koch, along with his brother, believes in philanthropy and giving back to the community. One of their charities is dedicated to cancer research. This cause is most likely very close to David Koch's heart, having survived cancer himself. Over the years, David has donated an incredibly large amount of money – over $100 million – to an MIT-run cancer research institute. These sizable donations help to fund scientists who are working toward breakthroughs. In the future, it's entirely possible that one of these scientists may move us closer to the ultimate goal – a cure.

David Koch is one of the most important people in the world because of his leadership of a massive, privately-run company, his understanding of diversification and the generous way he donates his money.

3 Reasons Why Knowledge is Essential

What do we stand to gain by knowing things? Take a look at some of the most successful people throughout history for the answer to that question: Abraham Lincoln, Henry Ford, Steve Jobs, Maya Angelou, Steven King and the list goes on. They all succeeded at their craft because they were highly knowledgeable in their field, as well as in life.

Knowledge is essential to success. It's a key component that drives people to succeed because the more knowledgeable an individual is, the more difficult it becomes to sit idly by and not put that knowledge into action. Knowledge often begets action. This is why having an educated community is essential to the improvement of any society. It all starts by picking up a book. Reading is a window into other worlds which allows people to gain essential knowledge, vicarious experience, imagination, creativity and much more. Here are three reasons why knowledge is essential.

Reason 1: Knowledge is power

Never forget that true power stems, not just from *knowing* things, but the way in which we utilize that knowledge. Conversely, ask yourself, what becomes of the uninformed individual? He is powerless to change his situation. Information is the cornerstone of change in both individuals and in society, and only by *knowing* things will we gain the power to change things.

How will you use your power of knowledge? At 3 Reasons Why, we believe in using knowledge to empower people everywhere. That's why we're hosting a series of events with knowledgeable guest speakers. Find the next 3RW event near you at events.3reasonswhy.com.

Reason 2: Knowledge is infectious

Have you ever learned something that you just had to share with another person? Knowledge is a fire that burns within us, begging to be released and spread from one person to the next. That is our mission here at 3RW – to spread knowledge to as many people as possible on as many topics as possible. Visit www.3ReasonsWhy.com and start spreading more knowledge today.

Reason 3: Knowledge is the remedy

Knowledge is the cure to poverty, because informed individual has an endless array of skills at his disposal which he uses to earn his keep. Knowledge is the cure to violence because the informed individual knows that there are alternative ways in which a conflict can be resolved. Knowledge is the cure to hunger, because the informed individual is resourceful and can find sustenance even in the harshest conditions. Knowledge is the remedy to most of life's little problems.

The world we live in is constantly in flux with an endless ebb and flow of information, all of which are made up of reasons that are ripe for *knowing*. As you walk down the crossroad of life, striving endlessly towards knowledge, there will undoubtedly be plenty of noise along the way. It can be easy to get distracted by the noise, but it is the task of every knowledge seeker to do their best to ignore that noise and find 3 simple reasons for everything.

Thank you or reading *The 3 Reasons Why Book of People*. If you enjoyed this book, you can find more reasons for just about everything at www.3ReasonsWhy.com. You can find more books like these available at books.3reasonswhy.com. Go forth and spread knowledge to the world.